LAST WILL, LAST TESTAMENT

LAST WILL, LAST TESTAMENT

Poems by
Frank X Walker

Accents Publishing • Lexington, Kentucky • 2019

Printed in the United States of America

Accents Publishing
Editor: Katerina Stoykova-Klemer
Cover Photo: Frank X Walker

Library of Congress Control Number: 2019937298
ISBN: 978-1-936628-49-0
First Edition

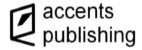

Accents Publishing is an independent press for brilliant voices. For a catalog of current and upcoming titles, please visit us on the Web at

www.accents-publishing.com

CONTENTS

For Wanda, Debra, Beverly, and all survivors of father loss;
and for those of us still in recovery.

In a family of secrets, he who asks hard questions sounds like a gun.

FOREWORD

It is said that when the big trees fall in our lives, they leave even bigger holes. When I became old enough, I struggled to build a relationship with a father who was an invisible man for most of my young life, and what we eventually managed to carve out still felt incomplete at his passing. My wife gifted me with a new son about three months before my father made his transition. In fact, the day she went into labor, I received a call that my father was also in the hospital. These poems were born out of the cauldron churning every possible high and low a person can feel when it comes to navigating the woodland of life and death. I offer this opening poem, "Botany," as a foreword, because I think it captures how big, how old, and how intertwined the roots of living and dying can be.

BOTANY

for Kumasi

The wagon had one good wheel,
but the mare was strong headed.
And the seed was new.

The plow was a bit rusty,
but the soil was dark and rich,
so we toiled in moonlit fields
whose faces sat open like books,
squinting up at the sky
until the forecast said   son.

We tiptoed around love's land mines,
measuring everything twice
before throwing caution to the wind,
smiling 'I do's and building a future
with all the broken pieces of our lives.

We will sit up all night in these fields
if we must, watering the earth
with prayers and tears,
giddy at each of your big, little kicks
and premature attempts to escape.

Hands palming the horizon of your navel,
we practice patience, throw salt and lime
at our fears. And we weed.
And we hoe. And we wait
and we wait   and   we   wait.

Eyes, closed. Hearts, open.
Minds, clear.
Like the good black farmers
who birthed us are wont to do.

ECLIPSE

This troika

a sun   and a moon
and a planet

three Black Russian nesting dolls

a Father   a Son   and a man
almost a Ghost

the beginning   middle   and end
of a complicated drama
gather here   smiling.

It is not something
spoken aloud,
but the entire room witnesses
them holding each other
with the same starlit, almond eyes,
the same wringing
oversized hands.

They all understand
this rare celestial alignment
will only happen
once   in their life time.

WHEEZE

The new one is full of mucous
and has not yet learned to breathe
through his mouth.

The old one is doing his best
with one lung
collapsed under the weight
of a mass of cancer.

In the wee hours on the hospital ward
and in our bedroom nursery,
I listen to them struggle to live.

One needs saline drops
to cut through his blockage.
The other hacks and coughs
until something thick and wet
is hauled up the well of his throat.

A blue rubber bulb will reach deep
into the nasal cavity and perform
a much-needed *opening of the mouth* for one.
A breathing treatment and oxygen tank
can pretend to be a lung for the other.

Holding my own breath,
I lie or sit here listening to my guys
gasp and wheeze and wish
all my worry   was air.

NIGHT SHIFT

Listening to daddy play dodge ball
with the sandman
is like holding vigil over our newborn
during his first night at home.

Except here, on the cancer ward,
the coveted days that can become weeks
and then hopefully months
don't automatically accumulate.

The hacking and coughing and beeping
that drift in from the other rooms
interrupt even the best of short sleeps
not already broken by nurses
and attendants checking vitals,
giving breathing treatments, adjusting IV drips,
dispensing meds, waking him only to ask
how he's been sleeping and if he needs anything.

He's patient, a skinny reclining Buddha.
I would've already said what his eyes are saying,
"I need yal to leave me alone and let me sleep"
at least for a couple of hours.
But instead, he just smiles like our baby.

PRACTICING MODESTY

He sneaks the urinal
into the bed each time
or waits for his daughters
to leave the room.

He refuses to wear
the ass-out hospital gown
and has a plastic bag
of his own pajamas
stacked bedside
and ready to wear.

He requests a cup
to secure his dentures
between meals and signifying.

The cancerous mass was heavy
enough to collapse his lung
but not his witty comebacks.

Despite the army of loved ones
wanting to hold him here,
he seems to be evaporating
before our eyes.

Staring at his hollowing body,
I ask where is the rest of him.

His eyes weigh the air
as he assesses possible retorts
and settles for, "wherever he is
he's doing better than me.
I'm in the hospital.
At least he was smart enough
to stay home."

HARVEST TIME

Cancer came
on quiet possum feet
disguised as pneumonia,
until the steady hack and cough
just wouldn't go away.

Everybody but him had forgotten
that he smoked
two packs a day for fifty years.

When he added up the cost,
realized he could buy that tiller
he wanted   in a month,
he took his last puff
and quit   without blinking.

If only he could use it
on the tension in this room
and plow up the nastiness,
mistrust, and division
rooted in the dirt
from a past he can no longer
turn under the ground.

HOOFERS

Catching up with the three of us
was less awkward than the slow dance
the two of us have done
for fifty years.
Maybe because the music was different.

Instead of the slow, heart-aching
waiting-for-you-to-say
'I love You' ballads
that always play
in the movie version of us,
the air is filled
with lyrics to children's songs.

You stare at a brand-new grandson
with a wide grin,
perhaps looking for
your trademark eyes
and wry smile.

I stare at you and imagine
you're looking back at me,
across time,
barely two months old,
tiny hands still learning to grip,
choosing to smile
at dance partners
by the amount of light in their eyes.

We drove a long way to make sure
this moment happened.

I waited even longer
to be sure   I'd seen it before.

LION KING

(the role of the herd of wildebeest
will be played by Keytruda)

We had fantasized
about such a gift, as him,
had even projected backwards
to imagine how many more
we might have had
instead of books and degrees
had we only met sooner.

We didn't plan it so much
as we did absolutely nothing
to prevent it, preferring to believe
that babies come when they are ready
and not when you think you are.

The birth of my dad's cancer
arrived in a similar fashion.
The only surprise
to him was that the doctor thought
the dark mass on his lung
was just pneumonia, until it grew.

His response, over the years,
to our urging him to quit was always,
"well, you gotta die from something."

But immunotherapy is no Plan B
and chemo is like a clothes hanger
in the hands of a man more invested
in making the kick-off than doing no harm.

WAIT, WEIGHT, DON'T TELL ME

> "He who does not prepare his children
> for his own death has failed as a father."
>
> —King T'Chaka

My new one is piling on the fat,
encouraged by good, warm breast milk
gulped so fast he often forgets to breathe.

Our antecedent, my father, is losing weight
even faster, threatening to disappear
before the spreading cancer can catch up.

My son is all curves and soft pinch-me flesh
with fingers as wide as miniature hot dogs.

My father's clavicle almost breaks his skin,
mandible much less prominent without dentures,
and the only round thing, the hollow in his cheeks.

They are wasting nothing and wasting away,
a beautiful beginning and an ugly end

with me at the fulcrum, trying to balance them both.

MEATPACKING PLANT

Each time I leave him,
trying to chase away
these new images of a body
fading before me
like an old photograph,
I reach for the before him,
cigarette cocked,
his body a young gun,
him in the long rubber apron
and boots,
blood and water everywhere,
a frozen me glancing up
and over his shoulders
at gigantic skinless slabs
floating on hooks,
the sound of machines and men,
and pigs and cows
being made into meat.

There is no effort
to disguise what they do
at the slaughter house,
nor does he explain.

People say cows are dumb,
but I have peered
into the backs of trucks
arriving from the stock yards
and nearby farms.

There's a look in the eye
before the last gate opens,
revealing a discomforting urgency

to choose
between lumbering headfirst
onto the killing floor
with panic   or with glee.

THE WHITE VERSION OF MY DADDY

Somewhere in a Danville, Kentucky
there's an 80-year-old white man
who was so angry
about integration
and so against change,
that he, too, vowed to quit school
before he'd share his space
with *them.*

He, too, turned his back
on science, and history,
and things in books
like cardinals mate for life,
male seahorses carry their young,
and the emperor penguin sits on
and hatches the egg.

He, too, would never know
that Canada, the Gulf of Mexico,
or the Atlantic were only two states
away when he dropped out
in the 8th grade
and put on his permanent blue collar.

His world view never stretched
further than his old Ford truck
could leap on one tank of gas.

He stopped worshipping
Adolph Rupp's basketball in '66,
started cussing the TV
when Rick started five of *them,*
and stopped watching
when they gave Tubby Smith the reins.

He's happy to be taking his leave
now that a man,
no whiter than him,
is fixing things
and making America great   again.

DREAM

We surrounded his bedside,
filled every inch of the room
with his generations,
with his progeny.

Perched on each other,
we carried everything
we thought he would need
in the afterlife
in our hearts
into what felt like
his burial chamber,
and placed it at his feet.

Tears rolled down his cheeks
as his eyes roamed
from face to face,
while we sang
and prayed in unison
like a flock of brown-eyed ravens
standing wing to wing,
honoring our humble beginning,
plucking feathers from our own bodies,
adding them to the pillows
beneath his head
until he was almost up right
and regal and laughing   again.

BILL COLLECTORS

Here we come again,
barging loud and proud
into the room by twos and threes,
dragging our brood along
to lay eyes on their own
living history,
believing that the awkwardness
will eventually turn to dust.

We have stood like guests
in sitting rooms
saturated with unconvincing
family portraits,
to introduce you
to your grandchildren,
to look you in the eye,
to just exchange   hellos,
until the suffocating silence
chased us back to our cars.

Your then-wife always flitted about,
almost afraid to be out of earshot.

But they all seem alarmed this time.
They do not welcome our presence.
It is as if we have come for something
that belongs to them and them alone.

But we only want to hear the stories
we were too young to know,
something of that bliss
that gave birth to us,
back when it was you who tucked us in
at night, back when *she* was still alive.

We have not come for cars or houses.
We have our own.
But we do want the memories you owe us.

WE BURIED HIM SITTING

When we visited
another "one last time,"
we crowded into his bathroom
in the order we were born,
stood close enough to touch
and pretended his shit didn't stink.

He looked up
as if only to confirm our identities
or match the faces
with the voices and the feet.

Void of all dignity,
his frail body
all but screaming surrender,
he grants us an audience
that leaves us wishing
we hadn't needed
to give it one more chance
to heal itself,
another chance to say
"good bye" and "we love you,"
to his face
and hopefully hear it back.

He was mostly skin and bones,
less than a fraction of the man
we thought we knew.
He refused our final attempts at humor,
and shrugged off our offers
of fulfilling items on his list
by simply saying
"Ain't nuthin' I can do with a bucket, now."

NO NAMES, KNOW NAMES

"May Our Father watch over my father"

—Common

I have carried your name and face
across the globe,
into galleries and classrooms,
auditoriums and stages,
and splattered it across newspapers
and television screens.

Though I replaced (y)our original middle name
with an X, a sacred journey
I began myself, to search for the unknown,
to declare how much
I didn't know about you,
about us, I am still Junior,
still the II, but the very first   son.

Smiling like the sun, I introduce myself
to your oncologist
then ask a thousand questions on your behalf,

but I can't speak for you,
I can't put words into your mouth.
Your rural Kentucky clicks and grumbles
don't translate
into audible 'I love you's or apologies,

even the ones we are dying to hear,
even to the ones who brought you here to die.

DRIVING IT LIKE IT WAS STOLEN

"We been together fifty-seven years, and we
gonna be together forever."

—Wife Number 2

The number struck me as odd
when it was first lobbed across
the hospital room, towards the end
of her dramatic performance
for anyone in our captive audience
who might have doubted
the authenticity or sanctity
of their love and marriage.

I was stunned. Not necessarily
because she held it up like a trophy
but for the fact that I had just turned
fifty-seven, and my younger sister,
his daughter, was fifty-six.

Those of us who could do the math
looked at each other to confirm
what we thought we had heard,
nodded and raised our eyebrows.

It was also at this point
he stopped letting her hold his hand,
like a disgruntled or embarrassed accomplice
who had just heard his partner-in-crime say:
"I didn't steal no car officer. It was sitting
in the parking lot unlocked with the keys
in the ignition, and everybody knows
possession is nine-tenths of the law."

THUMB WRESTLERS

We held hands for the first time
on his deathbed, which would have been
insignificant had we at least shared
a fist bump, some dap, or a ritual
handshake during any of our times together.

The distance between us always felt
wider because of the unspoken rule
about unsolicited touching. According
to his sister, people always thought
he was a loner, but he was just "private."
So in his hospital room, surrounded
by unblended families,
I leaned in close and whispered,
then he squeezed and I squeezed back.

It was the loudest conversation
we had ever had. My warm breath in his ear,
our large twin hands entwined and grappling,
inventing our own Morse Code,
shouting all the things
we never found words for.

We held hands for the first time
on his deathbed, but I imagine an infant me,
wrapping all my tiny digits around the expanse
of one of his massive thumbs, like my son
is doing now.

SWEAT EQUITY

for Maurice Walker

You must have known
I needed to feel close to him.
So we dug holes,
mixed and poured
wheelbarrows of cement,
planted posts,
and conversed more with sweat
than words
until the evening sun called it quits.

For days, I sweated through my clothes
carrying boards, sawing, hammering,
marking and measuring,
then we paused,
pyramid builders
raising something grand
out of the desert, out of the mud
in your backyard.

Of all the grandsons,
you look most like my father,
especially with a cigarette
balanced on your lips
and a pencil behind your ear.

Earning these calluses,
performing
his version of an honest day's work,
coaxing your new deck
out of the ground,
allows me to imagine

I'm building a temple with him,
something broad and enduring,
that could be witnessed
for miles and miles,

like his laughter,
like both of your smiles.

ANSWERING MACHINE

I appreciate your condolences
and prayers.
Many heartfelt thanks
for the beautiful flowers,
cards, and hugs.

But just let me breathe today.
Let me linger in bed
for as long as I want.

Let me have some fresh air.
Let me walk and moan
and wail and cry alone today.

Let me get down in the mud
and wallow in this pain.
Let me break bread
with all this hurt
and really build some trust.

Offer your covered dishes
and good tidings to another.
Check on, comfort, and try to dry
someone else's tears today.

I'm not saying I don't need your
'everything will be all right's
or prayers.
I'm not saying I'm okay.
All I'm saying when my eyes
go straight to voice mail
is: I'm not home right now.

Please leave a message
while I grieve. I'll get back to you
after all these … beeeeeeeep.

BECAUSE IT'S A FUNERAL

"Honour thy father and thy mother ..."

—Ten Commandments

I know I'm supposed to follow
everybody else's lead,
stand here with tears in my throat,
lamenting his passing,
and talking about what a great man
and a great father he was.

But what is the child to do
when telling the truth sounds like
disrespect of the father, and telling a lie
dishonors a mother
who preceded him in death,
who might have lived longer,
who may have had a better life
if not for some of the choices
they both made?

I liked my father the person,
even when he was throwing shade
and being witty you could hear
how smart and wise he was.

He didn't waste time on dreams, books,
or big ideas. He never flew in a plane.
Never saw the ocean. Dropped out of school
in the 8th grade to work.
Was never afraid of long hours or sweat.
He was non-confrontational. Too much
to join the army like all his brothers.
He didn't want to see the world.
Had seen enough pain by the end of his divorce.

Didn't care much for church.
He was quite happy on his knees in a garden,
underneath an old car or truck,
piddling around with junk he picked up
on the side of the road.
Dr. Frankenstein of the tool shed.
Attracted to any and every broken thing,
maybe to give his life some purpose,
perhaps to compensate for things
he felt he couldn't fix.

People thought him a quiet man.
Perhaps his almost monastic silence,
was self-imposed penance for language
he didn't own or at least express.
No "I regrets," "I made some mistakes,"
or "I still want time with my kids."

I won't dishonor him here today.
I *am* sorry he's gone. Or rather,
I wished he had lived long enough
to help make some of this right.

But I am grateful for his anti-lessons
on how to be a great father, for teaching
me that presence is more important
than presents, and how to raise children
with so much care that they never hear
or use words like *step*-sister or *half*-brother.

Let my father's life be an example
to all of you who might marry someone
with children. If you knowingly and lovingly
make that commitment, let it be simple math

with whole numbers. Not subtraction.
Not substitution. Not competition.
And no half anythings. Just more.
More children. More siblings. More love.

THE REAL CREATOR

Though your funeral was in a church,
your cathedral was the great outdoors.

Work was your religion.
You paid your tithes in sweat.

You didn't trust the sanctified.
You were pretty sure stained-glass windows
were used to keep people from looking inside.

Yet, you believed   in something,
figured that whatever made us,
whoever could put an oak tree
inside an acorn or transform a moment
of orgasmic pleasure into a brand-new life
with its own purpose
and powerful new engine
that would eventually get old
and wear out
like all good things,
would be too big   to fit   inside a book.

WINTER IS COMING

> "Tears aren't a woman's only weapon …"
>
> —Cersei Lannister

The new wife was a hot young thing,
which tormented my mother and her
three-kids-too-quick body, soon robbed
of its svelte waistline and narrow hips.

Something not-good-witch and ever-plotting
about her, still, around the eyes and fake smile.

Every formerly mousey thing has aged
into rodent: the scurrying, the false modesty,
the hiding in the corner of the room.

She used to linger just outside the doorframe,
monitoring every word when we came to visit,
tried to raise her kids as the only true heirs,
like a monarch in the *Game of Thrones*.

A premature wake for an ailing patriarch
has begun. The war of attrition is next.

ALL HE LEFT US WAS A LOAN

It seems that our papa
was a rolling stone.

Not a rock and roll legend
and nothing like the one

rolled in front of the tomb,
though just as quiet.

He was just enough like the song
the Temptations sang

for my sisters to break out
in three-part harmony

after comparing
all our birthdates,

but mama never said
bad things about him.

He worked
almost every day of his life.

He didn't have three outside children
like the papa in the song, only one.

He was a jack of all trades,
but never begged, borrowed, or stole.

Despite his obituary,
he never went anywhere near a church.

Maybe I collected hats because
of wherever he laid his.

It is true however that when he died
all he left us was alone.

Though that line didn't hurt as much
when we thought we were singing it right.

SOME ASSEMBLY REQUIRED

"Supposed to have leftover nuts and bolts,"
he said, every time he assembled something
without reading the instructions.

"It don't have to be perfect as long as it works,"
was his mantra, according to the oldest son,
he raised,
something he said after ripping up the hardwood,
trying to put it back together, and being unable
to determine if it was the wall or the floor
that was crooked.

Barbed wire fence and a territorial new bride
protected a prosperous garden
carved into the edge of a well-manicured lawn,
separating working class Harding Street
from the projects,
dividing the haves from the stomach knots.

Now, an even sharper wire divides the kids
he raised in their own yard
from the ones he didn't finish building.

But while the garden side crafts a eulogy
unburdened by the past, the project kids
keep reaching for their missing screws.

SECONDS

I believe what *she* refers
to as his meanness
is something pickled in regrets,
something soaked in a lye-filled
tub of second guesses,
like lying down with her,
starting a second family,
needing a fifty-plus-
year-long cloud of smoke
to taste good memories.

All made more real
by being given a second chance
to be sought after for advice,
to be loved and celebrated
on Fathers' Day and again a month later
on the anniversary of his birth.

But watching him shrug off
the possible consequences
of decades of two packs a day,
surrendering to her,
to death itself,
helps us understand
that he was just too ornery
to ever admit he was wrong,
too hard-headed for apologies,
and way too regretful
all those years to allow himself
to really love again,
which, maybe, might come across
as mean.

BECAUSE I LOOK MORE LIKE MY FATHER

> "My mama thinks you don't like her."
>
> —That Other Sister

Is it the way I still carry this torch
for my mother,
for the woman who birthed, loved,
and nurtured me,
for the woman who committed
the rest of her life
to filling up the hole
our father's absence created?

Is it because I don't return
her fake smile?
Is it the smirk on my face
that says I still remember
the color of her lipstick,
and the lie on her lips
through the screen door
despite your watery urges
for us to forget the past?

I imagine protecting
what she decided
was hers alone,
included us not knowing
you or your brothers existed,
or not being familial-minded
enough to insist he participate
in the lives of the first kids
he brought into the world,
instead of just replacing them
with three of her own.

MR. MIAGI

My life has become a parody
of the Karate Kid, except instead
of "wax on, wax off,"
I'm folding onesies, tiny socks
that look more like finger puppets,
small towels with cute little
animal faces, and bibs.

After watching a stack
of miniature wash cloths
almost disappear and swell
at the same time,
I finally discern the lessons.

All these years I thought
of my parents' divorce
as a family being halved,
a father losing a son.
What I didn't see
is when he folded and put us away,
something about us became thicker
and more absorbent.
We were still all there,
though we often felt a little bit smaller.

I imagine them folding that last diaper
like a dead soldier's flag,
but no twenty-one-gun salute, no bugle call,
just a hole big enough to bury something
and some body left behind to kick in the dirt.

GHOST DAD

Shaggy, Scooby, and my Pops
taught me everything I needed
to know about haunted houses.

To be terrorized by feelings
of inadequacy
every time the Ouija board
spelled out F.A.T.H.E.R.
was scary enough.

Behind every frightening apparition,
duppy, or monster
exists a much smaller man
made larger by our fears.

Mama nodded at the examples
set by Granddaddy Dave
and Coach P.
They helped put flesh and bones
on the invisible man
I could not hold or hug.

Their strong hands and approving smiles
pointed the way, helped correct my path,
and made it easier to stop believing
in ghosts.

LAST WILL, LAST TESTAMENT

After you popped your teeth
back in, I realized
that I didn't know
you wore dentures.

Or maybe   I mean
I had no idea for how long,
and had never seen you
without the half smile
you allow folks
except when you've said
something so funny
you have to surrender a full grin
and laugh too.

I felt the same thing
when I used your bathroom
and saw the opened package
of Depends on the floor,

and again when the nurse
sat you up in bed for a bath
and I saw the sunflower-sized
cluster of moles
in the center of your back
and reached for my own.

We arrived at this moment
closer than where we started,
but all the tension crowding
the unblended families
into this too-tiny hospital room
has revealed how far apart
we all remain.

They may have gotten the houses,
the cars and the money,
but I got your face   and your name.

PISSING ON PRIMOGENITURE

To use a loved one's sickness and death
to wield perceived power was just a ruse.

Pretending to be the first or only heir
did not make it true.

Twisting an innocent joke into a paternity test,
defending an answer that had never been questioned,
then clouding my sister's legitimacy
seemed Trumpish to me. He also liked to insist
his competition was guilty of his own crimes.

Always seeing yourself in somebody else's shadow,
choosing to parrot maternal lies,
knowing all you know, believing nobody else does,
and given all that you conspired to hide or erase
out of loyalty, out of honor   must have been tough.

And we thought growing up without a daddy was hard.

OBITUARY

My Anger died on Friday, July 13, 2018.

It was born in the '60s.
It succumbed after a prolonged dis-ease.

It is survived by well-honed character
and class, a sense of humor,
and a host of other emotions,
including grief, several grand griefs
and a flock of great grand griefs.

Multiple services are scheduled.

Last rites will be held inside a book of poems,
mixed in acrylic paint and spread on canvas,
and poured in the creek in my sister's back yard.

The repass will be in my children's eyes,
my woman's arms, and on an 18th hole.

MAKING NEW MEMORIES

I went searching for a memory
of my father with his father,
but found only the one
of the two of them in suits,
mimicking a tree and the ground.

At the same funeral,
father's brother's hands
were steel-cuffed
at the wrists.

In the most recent double of them,
uncle, though no longer convicted,
is wearing a single-breasted casket too.

When I walked away
from my father's final repose
without a button-down shirt or cotton tie,
cradling a too-chatty son in my arms,

I wore an embroidered African shirt
fit for a king, and so did all my progeny.

I mean to break this cycle,
this ill-fitting tradition that hangs
European suits on the dead men in our line.

My sons have seen me standing over
my father's grave, regally attired.
When it's my time to rest,
I hope they remember what skins to wear
and which kente to wrap me in.

I want us sent off in the direction
from which we come, adorned like Ashanti,
Shango's drums opening the sky,
cowrie shells raining down
and singing like castanets.

THOU SHALT NOT UNFRIEND YOUR NEIGHBOR

for #facebookthugz

Maybe you have such empty lives you believe
your true friends are a click and a pew away.

But aren't you too smart to believe a few likes
and all-caps mean this bright bible is the truth?

When you see a Holy Ghost, nobody can hear you screen.
You are vociferous and braggadocios when preying.

You work so hard to elicit sympathy online
you even feel sorry and cross yourselves.

Overusing the emoticon for prayer
must give you the street cred you need.

Because you were raised without Faith
maybe Facebook *is* your church.

VENTRILOQUISM

"Paper will let you write anything on it.
Lies, poems, they all the same,"
is something my father allegedly
"ALWAYS said,"
before his untimely demise.
But it's easy to put words
in a dead man's mouth.

His quietness was legendary,
but he has been downright chatty
in the afterlife, spouting off about
which kids aren't actually his,
who could or couldn't have donated
an organ if he needed one,
expressing anger at a former lover
who visited in his last days,
banning his eldest son from
cancer treatments because
he asked the doctor too many questions,
screaming (with a collapsed lung)
at his sister over the phone
about said son disrespecting his *wife*
and acting like a king,
declaring which grandsons
he didn't want to carry his casket,
requesting a twisted birth order
and retroactive church membership
just for the obituary,
deciding which kids to disinherit
and how to carve his headstone.

Funny how he's had time to say all of that,
but nothing about *not* receiving
his at-home breathing treatments
or needing his oxygen turned up in the end.

IN ANOTHER UNIVERSE

You are seated at the head
of the table,
favorite wives on every side.

Your children, who take their cues
from their beautiful mothers,
smile and nod to each other
with kindness and respect.

After your prayer, you pass meat
and greens from the plenty,
break loaves of bread
into equal pieces,
and send them down both sides.

You unwrap story after story,
challenge us to find the lessons,
urge us to never forget
whose name we carry.

You teach and coach,
chide and praise,
before dispensing discipline
and laughter in equal measures.

Your father's generation
attended the funeral of the last racist.

Outside the president is not white
or male, neither is God.

Forgiveness is our new last name,
Loving is our first.

RITUAL

We migrate to the front stoop,
still in night clothes,
to stretch and greet
an end-of-summer sun
that peeks over the mountains
between tall trees
and across rooftops
to kiss his face,
to bathe my eyelids.

All the leaves, our flowers,
and almost every blade of grass
leans and reaches with us
towards the warmth.

He listens for morning sounds,
passing cars and buses,
cicadas, birds,
all already hard at work.

At sunset
we turn down all the lights,
put on soft music,
move much more slowly,
whisper,
reopen the blinds
and let sleep crawl in.

He closes his eyes
wrapped in the comfort of darkness,
learning that life
is what happens in between
son rise   and son   set.

MOURNING ... SUN

It is early morning
when his tiny hands clutch
their first leaf.

It is brown like us.

We both smile up
at the tree
and the invisible wind
that sent it.

As I hold him tight,
I wonder what he knows
about seasons,

how his arrival
gave my father
permission to leave.

ROCK, PAPER, SCISSORS

There is no scrum
in the treetops this morning.
The birds that have come
for the webworms all week
have been silenced
by the heavy rains.

My lil' caterpillar and I peek
through the blinds
and cock our heads
towards the sound
of the downpour
on the roof.
His eyes big up
when lightning flashes.

Fifty years of tobacco moths
laid eggs that hatched
as a many-legged chimera.
It grew inside my father
for months, transforming him
into a chrysalis.

But even alive he was as stoic
as a rock.
I exercised my grief
on paper,
and a newborn cut
much of the bitterness away.

AFROFUTURISTIC MESSAGING

When I hear him laughing
until he runs out of breath,
gulping more air and giggling again
at something unseen in the ether,
or catch him staring intently
over my shoulder
in the direction
of our Dogon masks
at something invisible
and possibly vibrating
in a spectrum of light only accessible
to the newly-arrived
or those about to depart,
I assume it is you   or mama
continuing one of the last and best
conversations you had on this side,
or exchanging coordinates.

He, barely a haiku, had just met you
and began jabbering and cooing
in couplets, like an old friend
from some other space and time.

You were even happier
to stare into familiar eyes,
to be comforted
about all that was ahead,
to catch up
with the old and the knew,
the breath between you
transforming into something
interdimensional,

the twinkle in your eye,
starlight
from another galaxy.

WHAT I THINK MY SON WAS TEACHING ME

To get what you want
in this world, you must
learn to crawl to it,
hope somebody
brings it to you, or be
strong enough to pull
it to yourself.

If you choose the independent route,
you might never know patience.

If you choose the lazy route,
you might never learn to walk.

If you choose
the muscular road,
make sure you understand
your own strength,
or you might just pull everything
down   on your head.

AUTUMNAL

Even though not unexpected
at this elevation, seasonal
colors come early.
The change arrives so quietly
few miss the green until its gone.

Like the cardinal
distracting the viewer,
the prettied-up foliage
will fall away,
exposing limbs, bones, truth,
fate.

You can surround a body at state
in a new suit of beautiful leaves,
but underneath floral scents
lives the finality of the end
of summers.

THE LESSON OF THE FALL TREES

after Lucille Clifton

the trees believe
such change is trust
such trust is strength
such strength is peace
such peace is love
I agree with the trees

AFTERWORD

MISSIVE TO FAITH AND FRANK

> "A person is not dead until the people
> no longer speak their names."
>
> —African proverb

I'm not sure how
interancestral communication
works, but I hope he had a chance
to tell you how he felt
when he came home
and you had taken us
and left him
with nothing but a twin bed.
Mama, I hope he has heard you say
explicitly why you felt
you had to take us and leave.

I hope you both felt heard.

You were new at parenting,
couldn't have known
how your actions
would impact us
for the rest of our lives.

But you birthed survivors
who still honor your choice
to bring us into this world.

Know that your children
understand loss all too well.
We now know what it feels like
to be both fleer and fled from.

We have clung to our own children
so tightly that the line is blurred
between generations.
Uncles and siblings,
nieces and grandmothers
have all tried to raise each other

to believe in love,
to believe in forgiveness,
to believe in family forever.

We wish you everlasting peace.
We will always speak   your names.

ACKNOWLEDGMENTS

I would like to thank the Creator for including me in the grand design, my ancestors both known and unknown for their strength and resilience, the community of poets, artists, colleagues, family, and friends that continues to nurture me, including Neil Chethik for his kindness and the gift of his beautiful and inspiring book *FatherLoss*. Many thanks to Katerina Stoykova and Accents Publishing for their early support of this manuscript and my work, and to my beautiful and brilliant wife, Shauna M. Morgan, who played midwife and disciplinarian to each of these poems as they began taking their first wobbly steps into the world almost a year ago, even before our gift of a new son took his. Thanks to her keen ears, eyes, and heart, these poems are so much stronger than when they first arrived.

ABOUT THE AUTHOR

The first African American writer to be named Kentucky Poet Laureate, Frank X Walker has published ten collections of poetry, including *Turn Me Loose: The Unghosting of Medgar Evers,* which was awarded the 2014 NAACP Image Award for Poetry and the Black Caucus American Library Association Honor Award for Poetry. He is also the author of *Buffalo Dance: The Journey of York,* winner of the 2004 Lillian Smith Book Award, and *Isaac Murphy: I Dedicate This Ride,* which he adapted for stage, earning him the Paul Green Foundation Playwrights Fellowship Award. His poetry was also dramatized for the 2016 Contemporary American Theater Festival in Shepherdstown, West Virginia and staged by Message Theater for the 2015 Breeders Cup Festival. A lover of comics, Walker curated "We Wear the Mask: Black Superheroes through the Ages," an exhibit of his personal collection of action figures, comics, and related memorabilia at the Lyric Theatre and Cultural Arts Center in 2015; he reprised the exhibit in 2018 at Purdue University and Western Carolina University.

Voted one of the most creative professors in the south, Walker coined the term "Affrilachia" and co-founded the Affrilachian Poets, subsequently publishing the much-celebrated eponymous collection. His honors also include a 2004 Lannan Literary Fellowship for Poetry, the 2008 and 2009 Denny C. Plattner Award for Outstanding Poetry in Appalachian Heritage, the 2013 West Virginia Humanities Council's Appalachian Heritage Award, as well as fellowships and residences with Cave Canem, the National Endowment for the Humanities, and the Kentucky Arts Council. The recipient of honorary doctorates from University of Kentucky, Transylvania University, Spalding University and Centre College, Walker is the founding editor of *pluck! The Journal of Affrilachian Arts & Culture* and serves as Professor of English and African American and Africana Studies at the University of Kentucky in Lexington.

OTHER BOOKS BY FRANK X WALKER

Eclipsing a Nappy New Millennium, Editor (1997)

Affrilachia (2000)

Buffalo Dance: The Journey of York (2004)

Black Box (2006)

America! What's My Name?, Editor (2007)

When Winter Come: The Ascension of York (2008)

Isaac Murphy: I Dedicate This Ride (2010)

Turn Me Loose: The Unghosting of Medgar Evers (2013)

About Flight (2015)

Affrilachian Sonnets (2016)

Ink Stains & Watermarks: New and Uncollected Poems (2017)